Summary and Analysis of

THE INNOVATOR'S DILEMMA

When New Technologies Cause Great Firms to Fail

Based on the Book by
Clayton M. Christensen

WORTH BOOKS

SMART SUMMARIES

This Worth Books book is based on the 2016 paperback reprint edition of *The Innovator's Dilemma* by Clayton M. Christensen, published by Harvard Business Review Press.

Summary and analysis copyright © 2017 by Open Road Integrated Media, Inc.

ISBN: 978-1-5040-4670-1

Worth Books
180 Maiden Lane
Suite 8A
New York, NY 10038
www.worthbooks.com

WORTH BOOKS
SMART SUMMARIES

Worth Books is a division of Open Road Integrated Media, Inc.

Contents

Context

Written in 1997, during the so-called tech bubble, and based on substantial research across many different industries, *The Innovator's Dilemma* was revised in 2000 and again in early 2016 to bring it up to date with emerging technology and new disruptions from entrants creating entirely new markets. While the majority of the case studies and examples focus on businesses in the late 20th century, they are more than relevant today—and there is much to learn from the successes and failures of the past that can be applied to tomorrow's innovations.

Based on research and multiple case studies, the book offers critical insight into what drives adoption of sustaining business development and what prevents organizations from successfully adopting disruptive practices. Though some of the industries and businesses may seem outdated to contemporary readers (8-inch drives and Woolworth stores), the fundamental principles that governed the successes or failures of different companies still resonate today.

Overview

In the early 1940s, Joseph Schumpeter introduced the concept of *creative destruction*, which he described in his book *Capitalism, Socialism, and Democracy* as "the process of industrial mutation . . . that incessantly revolutionizes the economic structure from within, incessantly destroying the old one, incessantly creating the new one. This process of creative destruction is the essential fact about capitalism."

In *The Innovator's Dilemma*, Clayton Christensen proves that disruptive technology is the force behind Schumpeter's concept of creative destruction. He does this with mountains of data taken from multiple industries and organizations to demonstrate that sound business management can actually sow the seeds of decline and eventual demise of companies of all stripes.

The dilemma is that doing the right things—listening and responding to customers, focusing resources on activities that maximize profit—are actually the wrong things when faced with disruptive technology. Christensen provides case study after case study that demonstrate these points and goes on to document the success stories of those who got the transition right and how others might follow their lead.

Summary

Preface

In this note to the reader, Christensen explains his reason for writing *The Innovator's Dilemma*. In 1990, he asked himself two questions that would shape the book: "Why is success so difficult to sustain?" and "Is successful innovation really as unpredictable as the data suggests?"

His graduate research led to some unsettling answers. First, it's often good management strategies that lead to a company's demise—listening to the customer and focusing on products that yield high returns. Doing the right thing can be the wrong thing.

To answer his second question, Christensen urges his readers to look at innovation as something that is inherently unpredictable, as opposed to a risk to be managed. With the help of data, we can more clearly read where innovation is going and which companies will fail and which will succeed.

The purpose of *The Innovator's Dilemma* is to help innovators, entrepreneurs, and investors know what to look for, what information to collect, what data to mine, and how to interpret that information so that they can predict and develop profitable services and products and run successful companies.

The Innovator's Dilemma is the result of years of research, tested and improved by hundreds of students, investors, innovators, consultants, academics, and executives. However, the theory of disruption can always be improved upon, and Christensen challenges each and every reader to continue the research in their own lives.

Introduction

The Innovator's Dilemma is about why great firms fail when faced with critical market and technological innovation. An example cited is Sears Roebuck, who introduced credit cards and mail order catalogs only to lose those markets to Visa and MasterCard, along with a long list of new catalog merchants.

The key principle regarding technological innovation is the difference between sustaining technology and disruptive technology. Well-managed companies routinely drive sustaining technological improvements, including incremental and breakthrough improvements, in their existing product lines. They are following sound business practices within the context of their organization, their customers, and the overall market for their products and services.

On the other hand, disruptive technologies are typically cheaper, simpler, and more user-friendly. They often enter at the low-cost, low-margin side of the market where larger organizations have limited or no motivation or even capability to step in.

Yet it is the disruptive businesses that capture new consumer segments and then start to move into the markets once owned by larger companies that, over time, leave legacy companies behind.

Part One: Why Great Companies Fail

How Can Great Firms Fail? Insights from the Hard Disk Drive Industry

Few industries have faced such a relentless march of performance improvements, sales growth, and market changes as the hard disk drive industry. In its nascent stage in the 1950s, it expanded with new players in the field over time. From 1976 to 1995, only one of the original seventeen leaders in the industry remained: IBM. Another 129 firms had entered the industry during this period, with 109 of those failing. This rapid turnover in technology and organizations, coupled with detailed market information published by *Disk/Trend Report,* made this industry a fertile field for exploring the central question of the book: How do great firms fail?

Clayton Christensen identifies two types of technological change: sustaining and disruptive. In the former, leading firms have always led the industry in implementing and commercializing sustaining innovations. However, with disruptive technology improvements, the opportunities and the market applications are so uncertain and so limited in size that only smaller entry-level companies consider them worth their time and money. Yet time after time, these smaller organizations are able to establish a market with their disruptive innovation and move up the value scale to take ever-increasing business from the existing organizations.

Sustaining technology improvements meet existing customers' needs with marked benefits, but ignore the needs of potential customers. Disruptive technology improvements are often at the low end of the market and typically find applications where the technology was not previously mechanically or economically feasible. They do not need to be massive breakthroughs, but are instead new applications in new or emerging markets.

Value Networks and the Impetus to Innovate

While some firms fail because of leadership or organizational issues, and others due to lack of experience with emerging technologies, here Christensen explains the concept of the value network and how it affects the potential for failure in established or legacy companies.

A value network is the framework of an organization established to create profit through its products and services. Consisting of people and technologies, it also forms the basis for the reward structure established within an organization. Think of a value network as all the physical components in a flat-screen TV or all of the parts that go into a microchip in the flat-screen TV. A value network may also be the manufacturers and markets involved in the business of smartphones, including customers, designers, advertisers, and salespeople.

If existing customers can't readily see the value of a disruptive innovation, they won't adopt it and the organization will most often drop it from their product development plans. Additionally, if the potential product does not meet the firm's standard cost structure, chiefly in terms of gross profit margin, it is not likely to be considered for further development.

All of these aspects serve to channel the resource allocation and investment decisions of the organization toward sustaining improvements that meet existing customer needs within existing applications. In these environments, disruptive innovations can't possibly make the cut.

The message here seems to be: Go outside of your existing customer base when exploring new product rollouts, and be aware of competition that might be coming from agile start-ups—even those that have not achieved any economy of scale.

Disruptive Technological Change in the Mechanical Excavator Industry

In this chapter, Christensen moves into a different industry, mechanical excavators, to examine the results of disruptive innovation and to demonstrate that these principles apply across many fields. In this case, the sustaining technology example is steam shovels that use cables to activate the machinery.

The sustaining improvements included moving from steam-engine power to gasoline-engine and then to diesel-electric power. He notes that twenty-three of the largest twenty-five manufacturers successfully made the transition to gasoline power.

The disruptive improvement was moving from cable to hydraulic actuators. Hydraulic actuators cannot match the lift capacity of cable actuators, which was the major sustaining improvement area for existing firms and their customers. Instead, makers of hydraulic actuators found new markets that valued their small size and high maneuverability. This included small residential contractors who used them to dig plumbing runs, basements, and foundations. These applications greatly cut their construction time in a niche that couldn't afford the time and cost of a major cable-driven mechanical excavator.

In this case study, the drive by existing firms in the mechanical excavator market was based on their value network of meeting the needs of existing customers and achieving profitability levels needed to justify sustaining improvements. As such, hydraulic activators didn't make sense. Yet new entrants in the field started with small markets, developed them, and then started to move upmarket to compete and excel where old-line firms once ruled.

What Goes Up, Can't Go Down

Here the case is made that organizations typically allocate resources toward proposed products that are expected to provide high margins and increased sales.

An example from the disk drive industry was that firms providing products to minicomputer manufacturers required gross margins of 40%. Those providing products to desktop computer makers needed 25%, while the mainframe market was used to 60%. Given these choices, those firms with already lower cost structures would be driven to move upmarket toward the higher margins. Never would they consider taking their higher cost structure to a less profitable market.

This seems to emphasize the point that what goes up, can't go down—especially when working familiar territory.

However, good managers will choose higher returns that can be capitalized upon from lower cost structures. They will recognize innovative ideas from any level within their organization and be open to funding the development of products and services that drive revenue from the lower end of the market, as in the case of minimill steel manufacturing (small, disruptive companies investing in technologies to providing low-end steel) versus integrated mills (large legacy companies with established consumers of high-end steel).

What Christensen demonstrates in this example is how established businesses, such as USX and Bethlehem Steel, have focused on creating internal efficiencies and cutting costs, while servicing the same high-end market they've always sold to, while newcomers—able to achieve similar cost-effectiveness out of the gate, while selling to consumers of low-end steel. The integrated mills were not interested in manufacturing bars and beams, and so the minimills were able to fill this market need and excel at it.

Part Two: Managing Disruptive Technological Change

Here Christensen suggests that good management is the root cause of organizational failure in the face of disruptive technology, which comes from making sound resource allocation decisions that address customer needs within their existing value network. The win will come to those companies that are able to shift the way they work and the way individuals and teams are evaluated.

Your organization may be destined to fail if:

- Your current customer base prevents innovation and experimentation.
- The potential for smaller markets are not recognized.
- A prospective use for a new product or service cannot be defined up front.
- Your organizational capabilities are too rigid for addressing disruptive change.

- There is hesitation about stepping in to emerging markets.

Successful managers harnessed these principles by:

- Aligning disruptive technology with customers who needed them.
- Placing the disruptive technology projects within organizations small enough to be excited and motivated by small wins.
- Learning through inexpensive experimentation and being open to early failures in identifying markets, products, and applications.
- Avoiding the larger organization's processes and values, instead using a smaller organization whose cost structure could be better aligned with these smaller opportunities.
- Finding or developing new markets rather than trying to wedge the disruptive technology into their main markets.

Give Responsibility for Disruptive Technologies to Organizations Whose Customers Need Them

The theory of resource dependence posits that an organization's freedom of action is limited to those actions that satisfy the needs of their customers and investors, who provide the resources the organization needs to survive.

Within this framework, disruptive technology that customers do not want and that investors won't support due to its unknown value is bound to fail. The alternative is to place the disruptive technology initiatives within an organization whose customers want the new technology and whose staff, processes, and resources value the small gains as they develop new products for new markets.

Case studies in this chapter include disk drive technology with spinoff and new organizations, discount retailing with gross margins that differ from traditional retailing, and laser printers versus ink-jet printers from two separate organizations within Hewlett-Packard.

Though it may seem counterintuitive, companies need to look beyond their current clients when deciding which initiatives should be funded.

An organization's value network must be aligned to support a disruptive technology. This can best be done by spinning off or launching new teams dedicated to a disruptive technology that's not connected to traditional resource allocation. This enables flexibility in development and resource dependence for an entity that can grapple effectively with the challenges inherent in finding and building new markets.

Match the Size of the Organization to the Size of the Market

In the world of disk drives, companies that entered disruptive value networks within the first two years were six times more likely to succeed than late arrivals. Unfortunately for large organizations, the early years of a disruptive market offer the least incentives for entry.

There are three ways for a large company to overcome this challenge:

1. Grow an emerging market big enough and quickly enough to make a meaningful difference to the overall revenue of the business.
2. Wait until the market is large enough to justify entry, but recognize that the likelihood of success for late entrants is much lower than for the leaders.
3. Assign disruptive technology to an independent team that's small enough to be motivated by early successes, and foster a culture where the early failures do not deter continued investment.

Discovering New and Emerging Markets

Disruptive technology finds and creates new markets. Since those new markets don't exist until they coalesce around the disruptive technology, they cannot be analyzed up front. They are, in fact, "unknowable." Within this context, traditional strategic business and marketing plans cannot be created. Instead, planning must be focused on a cycle of learning and discovery.

The first case study in this chapter focuses on Hewlett-Packard's development of a 1.3-inch disk drive for the emerging personal digital assistant (PDA) market as represented by the Apple in the early 1990s. The market for both the PDA and the drive didn't materialize. What did emerge were applications in miniature cash registers, cameras, and mass-market video game systems. But this market for disruptive technology demanded pricing at $50 per drive versus the $250 per drive unit that HP originally developed for the PDA market.

Additional case studies in this chapter included Honda's entry into the US motorcycle market, creating the disruptive market for small-engine off-road bikes, and Intel's introduction of the microprocessor.

The key concept is that markets for disruptive technologies emerge from unanticipated successes, and those are often preceded by failures. Hits can be made with the employment of discovery-driven planning with modest initial investments in trials to conserve resources, followed by adjustments to plans to take advantage of discoveries. It's ready, fire, aim in action.

How to Appraise Your Organization's Capabilities and Disabilities

How do you know if an organization is capable of successfully executing the work it is given? This assessment of people has been a hallmark of sound management practice, when followed by the necessary coaching and training, but business leaders seldom consider that organizations, too, have capabilities and disabilities.

To assess a company, and evaluate what it can and cannot excel at, consider the quality of its:

- Resources: This would include staff, intellectual property, physical space, equipment, finances, and the network in which it operates.
- Processes: Methods for producing value out of products or services, and running the business.
- Values: At the core of an organization, its values—when communicated widely—should influence how individuals prioritize and make decisions.

These same capabilities, which are the source of success for the organization, may also define what they cannot do. Imagine a business focused on sustaining or traditional technologies that has honed its people and processes in a particular way, and whose management team expects a certain return on their investment. This type of organization is unlikely to be flexible enough to change its people or processes to accommodate disruptive technologies, and is equally not suited to take risks associated with new models and markets.

Christensen suggests how to create *new* organizational capabilities:

- Acquire an organization that matches the task at hand.
- Try to change the current organization capabilities.
- Create a spinoff organization and instill the new values within it.

Performance Provided, Market Demand, and the Product Life Cycle

Performance oversupply occurs when a developed technology exceeds market needs, signaling a change in the basis of competition, and opens the door for disruptive technology to jump in.

This is shown within the product life cycle where there is a buying hierarchy that follows four distinct phases: functionality, reliability, convenience, and price. In the disk drive market, the early focus was on the functionality of capacity and physical size. As these were satisfied, reliability became crucial, and then price became the primary purchase motivator.

Case studies include Intuit's entrance into the accounting market and extending that to personal financial management software, and Eli Lilly's work improving the effectiveness of insulin. In the latter case, from 1925 to 1980 Lilly steadily improved the purity of insulin derived from animals. Then, at great expense, they created a 100% pure insulin produced with biotechnology priced at a 25% premium. Response in the consumer market was poor.

When Novo introduced a line of insulin pens for injection, they disrupted the status quo and turned what had been a two- to three-minute effort into one that took only seconds. Priced at a 30% premium, the product met with substantial success. This demonstrates that the sustaining technology's performance exceeded market demand, while the disruptive technology entered through being more convenient, and did so at a higher price.

Successfully implementing disruptive technology should be framed as a marketing challenge rather than a technology challenge. Disruptive technology seldom matches the capability of mainstream products. Instead, it creates new markets where its capabilities fit the potential application. It is typically simpler, more reliable, and convenient than existing technology, resulting in lower costs.

Managing Disruptive Technological Change—A Case Study

This chapter brings all the information presented in the previous chapters into play within a hypothetical case study focused on the development of electric vehicles. Christensen uses this industry to demonstrate how he might approach such a potentially disruptive initiative from inside an established automotive company.

The first step is analytical: Determine if a technology is actually disruptive by examining the current market and observing consumer behaviors. One would also need to determine if there is a path to moving from niche to mainstream use. If you discover that, over time, the performance of an electric car business could outpace (not just match) the "mainstream" market, you'll know that that the potential for disruption is there.

When considering defining a market strategy for your innovative endeavor, you'll want to keep simplicity and convenience in mind, as well as the ability to change direction as the marketplace shifts. And in any organization where resources (financial, technical, human) are limited, it is imperative to move beyond "rational resource allocation" to provide proper support for an emerging business.

The Dilemmas of Innovation—A Summary

Clayton M. Christensen provides a summary of the insights provided throughout the book, noting that they initially seem counterintuitive at first, but make sense after closer inspection, when they reveal themselves as simple and sensible:

1. The progress demanded by markets may be different from that offered by technology. Customers only know what they need today, not what they may need or want tomorrow.
2. Managing innovation is about resource allocation within an organization. Priorities will pick the winners and the winners will match the organization's existing value network.
3. Moving disruptive technology to market requires finding the market that values the technology.
4. Organizations have specialized capabilities and value networks that establish how they respond to opportunities. As a result, they are resistant to taking on disruptive change that requires a completely different value network.

5. Solid research about emerging markets and their reception of disruptive technology doesn't exist. Risk is very high and requires quick, inexpensive, flexible entry, followed by adjustments for new attempts.

6. "Blanket technology" strategies of always being a leader or a follower have limited usefulness when faced with the differences between sustaining and disruptive technologies. Leadership in disruptive technologies can offer significant rewards, while leading sustaining technologies offer fewer.

7. Established organizations have strong built-in barriers to entering disruptive markets, which can be a significant advantage for entrants to those emerging markets. This insight differs substantially from that traditionally offered by economists.

Company Directory

Apple Computer: Apple is credited with creating the personal computer market, but not without significant failures early on. They are likewise credited with launching personal digital assistants, but their Newton was considered a flop. Finding the right market for emerging and disruptive technology is the key.

Bethlehem Steel: Mentioned as an example of an integrated steel company that was disrupted by emerging minimills that took over the low end of their market in the 1990s.

Caterpillar: They were among a number of successful competitors in the excavation equipment manufacturing business that employed hydraulics technologies instead of relying on traditional designs.

Conner Peripherals: While larger, faster hard drives were the sustaining innovations in the disk drive industry, Conner Peripherals created small drives with less capacity and lower power requirements to better meet the needs of the emerging portable computer market.

Digital Equipment Corporation (DEC): A successful maker of minicomputers, it failed when faced with the emerging personal computer market. While it had the resources to compete in this market, its processes could not. The minicomputer design process required two to three years, while the personal computer market demanded six- to twelve-month cycles. DEC could not make the change to compete.

Eli Lilly and Company: They were the leading insulin manufacturer and relentlessly pursued sustaining product innovation. They felt the key for medical insulin was purity, which drove them to invest millions in producing 100% pure insulin. However, their customers weren't interested and lost market share to a small company called Novo.

Harley-Davidson: When faced with the insurgence of Honda's small motorcycles, they purchased Aeromecchania to compete. However, their dealer network rejected the smaller and lower-profit products as they didn't fit their businesses. While attempting to react to disruptive technology, their customers (dealers) prevented the change, nearly forcing the company into failure.

Hewlett-Packard: When faced with the disruptive technology of ink-jet printers that would compete with their line of laser-jet printers, HP created a completely autonomous business solely focused on ink-jet printers. In this way, it prevented its existing corporate values from rejecting the low-margin, low-cost disruptive technology.

Honda: They attempted to enter the US market with upscale motorcycles, but couldn't break through the existing competition. Instead, they discovered by accident that many customers were interested in their small bikes. Once focused on this disruptive technology, they created a new market and eventually moved upmarket to take on competitors such as Harley-Davidson.

IBM: They survived several waves of disruptive innovation to their mainframe computer business. Faced with minicomputers, they eventually started making their own as a defensive measure. With the advent of personal computers, they established an autonomous organization far away from headquarters, where it wouldn't be influenced by the existing corporate value network of high margin and high cost. Separately it could establish its own products, cost structure, and sales channels.

Intel: They moved from manufacturing dynamic random access memory (DRAM) to microprocessors, a disruptive technology that they invented. As this market grew, Intel's independently operated resource-allocation process provided more and more funds to microprocessors to help them scale up to meet the demands of a growing business.

Intuit: Through their product QuickBooks, Intuit captured 70% of the small-business accounting software market. They produced simple software that anyone could use and that didn't require a professional accountant. They changed the basis of competition from functionality to convenience.

J. I. Case: They built a market for small excavators that fit the needs of residential contractors, who valued mobility on residential lots to complete tasks that normally required manpower and shovels.

Johnson & Johnson: They match the size of the organization to the size of the market. With more than 160 individually operating companies, they can launch products with disruptive technologies to the markets that want them within organizations that value them.

Kresge: Recognizing the disruptive change of discount retailers, Kresge launched the Kmart chain. They successfully created a focused discount retail organization that was independent from their traditional business.

Micropolis: The firm made the transition from making 8-inch disk drives to 5.25-inch drives chiefly through the focus of its founder and chief executive, who had to completely transform the organization to move into the new market.

Novo: They realized that patients who required insulin would want an easier method than traditional syringe injections—and that they were willing to pay for this convenience. Their disruptive innovation, a pen-like device to administer insulin, ate away at Eli Lilly's market share.

Nucor Steel: Deploying minimills to enter the low end of the steel market, without much reaction from traditional competitors, they began to move upmarket to capture growing shares of larger bars, rods, and structural beams. Their lower cost structure and lower-quality steel ran many large integrated steel mills out of the business.

Priam: Led the market for 8-inch disk drives suited for minicomputers. However, their launch into personal computers and 5.25-inch drives failed because they maintained their two-year product development process, which fit the minicomputer market, but fell woefully short in the personal computer market.

Quantum: A leading manufacturer of 8-inch disk drives, a few of its executives sought to leave and start their own firm that would leapfrog the move to 5.25-inch drives by developing 3.5-inch drives. Quantum elected to spin off this venture with completely separate facilities and staff. As Quantum's sales slacked off over the years, the emerging 3.5-inch sales replaced them.

Seagate: As disk drives advanced from 8-inch to 5.25-inch to 3.5-inch, Seagate chose to stay with 8-inch drives and move upmarket with high-capacity products, addressing midrange computers such as file servers and workstations.

F. W. Woolworth: When faced with the disruptive innovation of discount retailing, Woolworth attempted to compete by introducing Woolco stores. They tried to run both their variety stores and discount retailers within the same organization. The two business models were not compatible within the same value network and their venture into discount retailing failed.

Direct Quotes
and Analysis

"It was as if the leading firms were held captive by their customers, enabling attacking firms to topple the incumbent industry leaders each time a disruptive technology emerged."

This gets to the heart of one of Christensen's key premises: that existing customers can prevent companies from moving into disruptive innovations because they can only see their own immediate needs. Instead, business leaders are counseled to seek out new customer bases, receptive to new ideas.

"The very decision-making and resource-allocation process that are key to the success of established com-

panies are the very processes that reject disruptive tech-
nologies: listening carefully to customers; tracking com-
petitor's actions carefully; and investing resources to
design and build higher-performance, higher-quality
products that will yield greater profit."

The focus of many excellent companies that follow logical business practices based on the needs of their current customers prevents them from implementing disruptive technology. Established business often see opportunities for new technologies and even develop their initial applications, but give up when the existing clients are not interested.

"Much of what the best executives in successful com-
panies have learned about managing innovation is not
relevant to disruptive technologies."

The development of *sustaining* innovations is often driven by customer desires and steady or even breakthrough improvements. Implementing *disruptive* technology requires an appetite to explore new markets, fail repeatedly, and develop relatively small, low-cost and low-profit opportunities that make use of the disruptive innovation—which may lead to success in the long run.

"The very mechanisms through which organizations
create value are intrinsically inimical to change."

Organizations create value through the optimization of their known processes and focus on an existing consumer base. These are precisely tuned to generate the necessary profit levels and product sales volume, but it prevents them from pursuing new customers in low-profit, low-volume emerging markets that have great potential to drive profit over time.

"To measure market needs, I would watch carefully what customers do, not simply listen to what they say."

Successful firms listen to their customers and build sustaining innovations to meet those needs. Disruptive innovation comes from watching customers closely and providing products that can revolutionize their application—things that the customer can't even imagine they need or want until they put them to use.

"The most powerful protection that small entrant firms enjoy as they build the emerging markets for disruptive technologies is that they are doing something that it simply does not make sense for the established leaders to do."

Large, established companies with their fine-tuned processes and known customer bases are often blind to disruptive innovation opportunities. And even when they can see applications for innovative technologies, most choose not to pursue the low-cost, low-volume opportunity that doesn't fit their business practice.

Trivia

1. The principles explored in *The Innovator's Dilemma* were inspired by Clayton M. Christensen's observation of the failure of Digital Equipment Corporation in 1988.

2. Market leaders often are the first to pioneer a new technology, but usually the last to recognize its significance. Seagate developed 3.5-inch disk drives and shared them with customers two years before Conner Peripherals shipped their first 3.5-inch drives. But Seagate's customers, desktop computer manufacturers, didn't want them at the time. Later, after 3.5-inch drives met the needs of their customers, Seagate finally entered the market, but it was too late.

3. The price per megabyte of a hard disk drive dropped by 5% each quarter from 1977 to 1994.

4. According to Thinkers50, Clayton M. Christensen is the #1 management thinker in the world.

5. You can take a course in "Disruptive Strategy" online with Clayton Christensen at HBX, a digital education channel of Harvard Business School.

6. The term "disruptive innovation" was coined by Christensen in 1995 in an article for the *Harvard Business Review*, "Disruptive Technologies: Catching the Wave."

7. The Clayton Christensen Institute is a not-for-profit organization founded with the mission of "improving the world through disruptive innovation."

8. In addition to being a global thought leader in business and economics, Clayton M. Christensen has also volunteered with the Boy Scouts of America for twenty-five years.

9. In addition to becoming a part of the lexicon of the spheres of business and technology, "The Innovator's Dilemma" is also the name of a multimedia art installation by German artist Simon Denny that was presented at MoMA PS1 in 2015.

What's That Word?

Disruptive technologies: Initially disruptive technologies underperform mainstream products, but they meet the needs of new markets because they are cheaper, simpler, and user-friendly. However, they offer small initial markets and lower profit. For these reasons, they are seldom motivating for large mainstream organizations.

Gross profit margin: A measure of financial success, gross profit margin is calculated by dividing gross profit by revenue; essentially, it is a ratio that expresses the profit made after costs are deducted from revenue derived from sales.

Innovation: A change in an organization's engineering and manufacturing as well as in their managerial, marketing, and investment processes.

Performance oversupply: Companies often focus on improving sustaining technologies instead of thinking about what will actually satisfy customers' needs. Performance oversupply occurs when a particular product has oversaturated the market, triggering a change in the basis of competition. For example: Previously, customers wanted high-performance disk drives and companies improved the 3.5-inch and the 5.2-inch drives until they were both provided adequate capacity. At that point, when the demand was satiated, other attributes become more important. Customers wanted smaller, nimbler machines, and were willing to pay a higher price for the 3.5-inch drives.

Resource dependence: In large, successful organizations, customers and investors control the allocation of resources, not managers. The most successful organizations are those that are proficient in killing ideas that customers don't want. This means that they cannot successfully implement disruptive technology, as it doesn't meet current customer requirements or desired profit levels.

Resources-processes-values (RPV) framework: The RPV framework is a tool to help explain a company's success in addressing sustaining vs. disruptive technologies. The industry leaders that develop and introduce sustaining technologies have the *capability* (resources and processes) to create disruptive technologies, but their values may not align with them (such as cost structures that do not accommodate lower margins).

Sustaining technologies: These are improvements in the performance of a product that meets the needs of current customers in mainstream markets. They can be incremental and breakthrough performance improvements. The key is that the improvement sustains the industry's rate of improvement by addressing the needs of current customers and markets.

Value Network: This is all those attributes and systems built within an organization to address customer and market needs. It's how organizations identify customer needs, solve problems, and build profit. It becomes the way the organization sees the world and, while providing value within their current network, blinds them to opportunities outside that network.

Critical Response

- A Global Business Book Award as the best business book of the year, 1997
- A *Fast Company* Leadership Hall of Fame book
- An *Economist* most important book about business

"Absolutely brilliant. Clayton Christensen provides an insightful analysis of changing technology and its importance to a company's future success."

—Michael Bloomberg,
founder of *Bloomberg BusinessWeek*
and former mayor of New York City

"*The Innovators Dilemma* achieves a rare feat: It is at once a satisfying intellectual solution to a long-standing business puzzle and a practical guide for executives and investors."   —*The Financial Times*

"*The Innovator's Dilemma* is one of the most—if not the most—important books chronicling how innovation takes place, and why its common that market leaders and incumbents fail to seize the next wave of innovation in their respective industries."   —*Wired.com*

About Clayton M. Christensen

In a poll of thousands of executives, professors, and consultants taken in 2011, Clayton Christensen was named the most influential business thinker in the world.

Originally from Salt Lake City, Utah, he earned a BA in economics from Brigham Young University, and an MPhil in applied econometrics from Oxford University, as well as an MBA and a DBA from the Harvard Business School.

A renowned and influential thought leader, bestselling author, professor, and speaker, he teaches "Building and Sustaining a Successful Enterprise" at the Harvard Business School and has founded successful businesses such as Innosight, an innovation consultancy, and the Innosight Institute, a think tank in the area of public policy.

For Your Information

Online

"Apple's Business Model Vulnerability, Exposed by a French Upstart." Forbes.com

"Clayton Christensen: 'Disruptive Innovations Create Jobs, Efficiency Innovations Destroy Them.'" TechCrunch.com

"Clayton Christensen: On Disruptive Innovation." ClaytonChristensen.com

"Clayton Christensen Wants to Transform Capitalism." Wired.com

"Clayton M. Christensen, The Thought Leader Interview." Strategy-Business.com

"Interview: Clayton Christensen on Disruption." CIO.com

"What Is Disruptive Innovation?" by Clayton Christensen, Michael E. Raynor, and Rory McDonald. HarvardBusinessReview.com

"When Giants Fail: What Business Has Learned from Clayton Christensen" by Larissa MacFarquhar. NewYorker.com

Books

Business Adventures by John Brooks

Crisis and Renewal: Meeting the Challenges of Organizational Change by David K. Hurst

Crossing the Chasm: Marketing and Selling Disruptive Products to Mainstream Customers by Geoffrey A. Moore

The Corporate Culture Survival Guide by Edgar H. Schein

Secret Formula by Frederick Allen

Ten Types of Innovation: The Discipline of Building Breakthroughs by Larry Keeley, Helen Walters, Ryan Pikkel, and Brian Quinn

The Lean Startup: How Today's Entrepreneurs Use Continuous Innovation to Create Radically Successful Businesses by Eric Ries

Winning Through Innovations: A Practical Guide to Leading Organizational Change and Renewal by Michael L. Tushman and Charles A. O'Reilly III

Other Books by Clayton M. Christensen

Competing Against Luck: The Story of Innovation and Customer Choice

Disrupting Class: How Disruptive Innovation Will Change the Way the World Learns

How Will You Measure Your Life?

The Innovator's Method: Bringing the Lean Startup into Your Organization

The Innovator's Prescription: A Disruptive Solution for Health Care

The Innovator's Solution: Creating and Sustaining Successful Growth

The Power of Everyday Missionaries: The What and How of Sharing the Gospel

Bibliography

Bower, Joseph L. and Clayton M. Christensen. "Disruptive Technologies: Catching the Wave." *Harvard Business Review*, accessed November 28, 2016, https://hbr.org/1995/01/disruptive-technologies-catching-the-wave.

Clayton Christensen website. http://www.claytonchristensen.com.

Cox, W. Michael, and Richard Alm. "Creative Destruction," *Concise Encyclopedia of Economics*. Library of Economics and Liberty. http://www.econlib.org/library/Enc/CreativeDestruction.html

Fisher, Lawrence M. "Clayton M. Christensen: The Thought Leader Interview." *Strategy + Business*, accessed November 28, 2016, www.strategy-business.com/article/14501?gko=ca7ad.

WORTH BOOKS
SMART SUMMARIES

So much to read, so little time?

Explore summaries of bestselling fiction and essential nonfiction books on a variety of subjects, including business, history, science, lifestyle, and much more.

Visit the store at
www.ebookstore.worthbooks.com

MORE SMART SUMMARIES
FROM WORTH BOOKS

BUSINESS

WORTH BOOKS

SMART SUMMARIES

OPEN ROAD

INTEGRATED MEDIA

Find a full list of our authors and
titles at www.openroadmedia.com

FOLLOW US
@OpenRoadMedia